DEDICATION

This book of Islamic poems is dedicated to my parents
Mr. Sabry Abdel-Aziz and Mrs. Azima Hamad Abdel-Aziz who worked very
hard to instill in my twin sister, Samar, and I love for Islam, even when
there were few Muslims around.

THANKS TO

My husband Dr. Hani Soliman
My children Ms. Hadeer, Mr. Siraj and Ms. Janna Soliman
New Horizon School Los Angeles principal, staff and students

All proceeds will go to an Islamic
educational institution.

Table of Contents

Preface

In 1998 when Christmas, Hanukkah and Ramadan were all celebrated during the month of December, I took my three children, 9-year-old Hadeer, 8-year-old Siraj and 6-year-old Janna to Story Time at the local library. With great excitement, the librarian told the wide-eyed children that she would read stories about the holidays in December to them: Christmas and Hanukkah. My daughter Hadeer, almost automatically, said to me, "How about Ramadan, Mommy? That's in December too." After Story Time was over I asked the librarian to share with the children a story about Ramadan too because all three holidays coincided this year. The librarian retorted, "Ramadan is not a fun month; it's a religious holiday."

I proceeded to tell her that like Christmas and Hanukkah, Ramadan is also a religious time and that it is, in fact, fun, just like those two holidays. After a long discussion on this matter the librarian agreed. If I could bring her a children's story about Ramadan she would share it during Story Time at the library. Naturally, I looked in the library for a children's short story about Ramadan. However, to my children's disappointment, and mine, there were none.

That is when I began working with my children on building off of their own experiences to write a story about Ramadan. I also designed an art project for the children to participate in during Story Time the following week at the library. Elhamdulilah, the following week we were ready with a story to share with the children and we made a lantern as the library's art project for the week.

The following year, when I started teaching and developing the Islamic Studies curriculum at New Horizon School in Los Angeles, CA, I asked my students to write short stories about Ramadan. I also requested that they write poems about the Quran, Ramadan, Eid, the Prophet Mohammad (pbuh) and thankfulness. I then worked on developing creative ideas for art projects to bring to life Islamic ideas and help us celebrate Islamic holidays.

Since our visit to the local library's Story Time, the library has provided me with a display window to showcase symbols, posters and facts about Ramadan. I hope my story will encourage other parents to work with their local communities and inspire their children to be proud of and to use their resources to develop their Muslim American identities.

Sahar Sabry Abdel-Aziz

The Quran

1

Quran

The Quran is a revelation from God to us,

We can even read it on the bus.

But we cannot read it in the washroom,

Or in the bathroom.

Another name for the Quran is the Furqan.

If there was no Quran there wouldn't be a Furqan.

It is the best source of knowledge and it gives us the most knowledge.

It has information on different subjects like believers and disbelievers,

And heaven, hell, Ismail and Israel.

By: Sumayya Hussaini

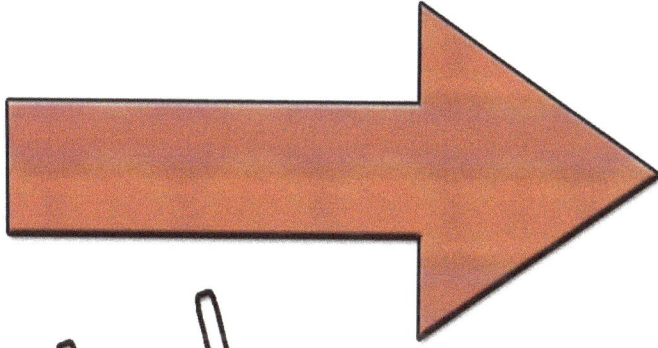

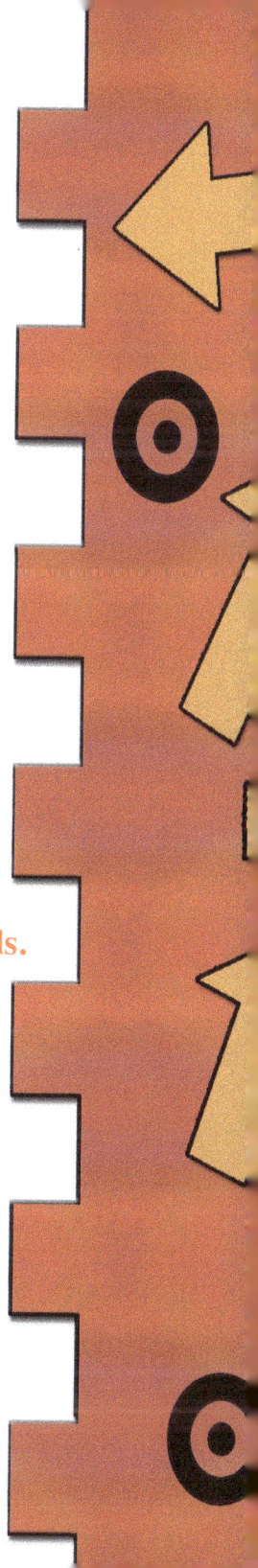

البيّنة

العصر

لقمان

2

<u>Quran</u>

The Quran is a guide for Muslims.

The Quran is a way of life for Muslims.

The Quran helps others convert to Islam because of its beautiful words.

By: Nabeeha Aleem

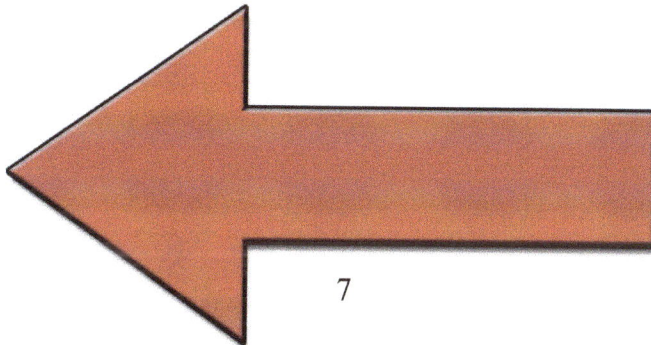

العاديات

3

What is the Quran?

The Quran teaches us how to live.

It teaches us to believe and to give.

The books given to the Prophets before Prophet Mohamed were not preserved.

But the Quran was to mankind served.

As the earlier books were lost or changed.

A Muslim follows the Quran and ordains.

The Quran is the best.

When you read it, you rest.

By: Hadeer Soliman

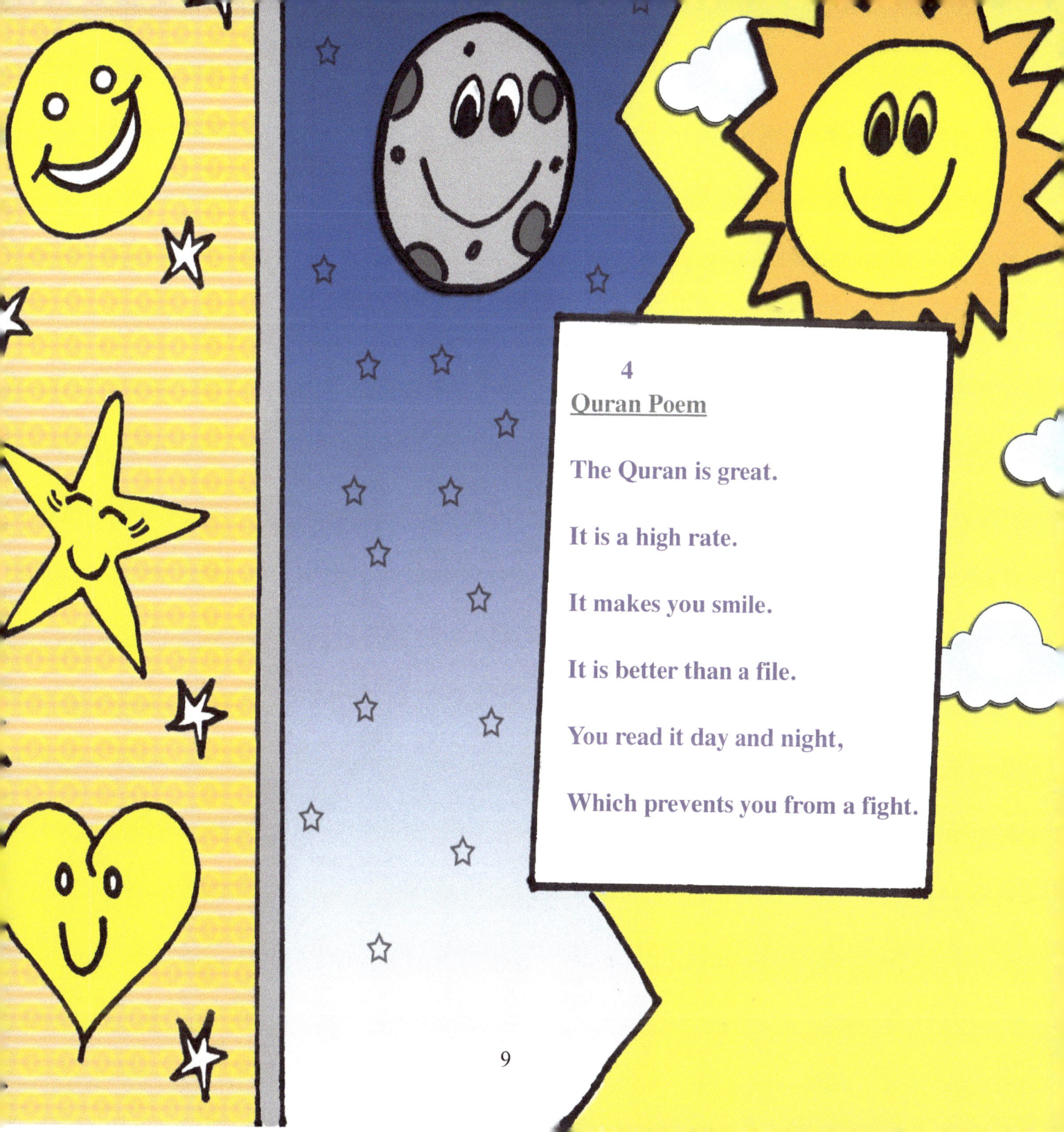

4

<u>Quran Poem</u>

The Quran is great.

It is a high rate.

It makes you smile.

It is better than a file.

You read it day and night,

Which prevents you from a fight.

5
Quran

Quilted with everything you need,
Uses things that which you feed.

Reading it is like a breeze,
Avoiding it will get you a bad deed.

Nothing is like it,
Nothing can beat it.

If you read it,
You will achieve it.

6
<u>The Quran</u>

The Quran contains a lot of information,
When you read it, it's a sensation.

"Read, read, read,"
That's what Angel Gabriel said.

Prophet Mohamed got scared,
And ran to bed.

"Cover me, cover me,"
That's what Prophet Mohamed said.

Thanks to the Quran,
Or you could say the Furqan,
Prophet Mohamed used this to let Islam spread.

7

Quran

Quran is love.

Quran is life.

Quran is in your heart and in your mind every day and night.

بِسْمِ اللَّهِ الرَّحْمَنِ الرَّحِيمِ

8

Quran Poem

Q is for Qiblah, where we face to pray.

U is for Ummah, which is the following of Islam.

R is for Rakat, which is part of the prayer.

A is for Ayah, which is in a Surah.

N is for Prophet Nuh, who is one of the Prophets of Allah.

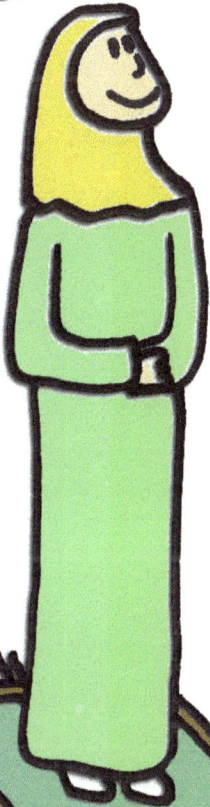

9

The Quran Poem

The Quran is preserved from the non-believers and reserved for the believers.

The Quran is the book of knowledge.

The Quran has verses and those verses are signs of Allah.

The Quran has another name separates right from wrong.

By: Sufian Hussaini

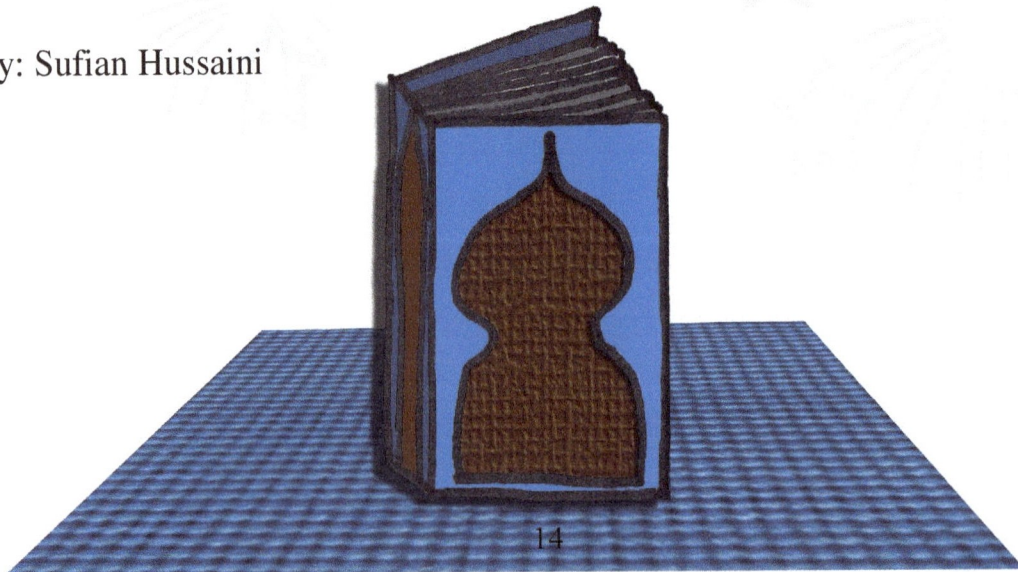

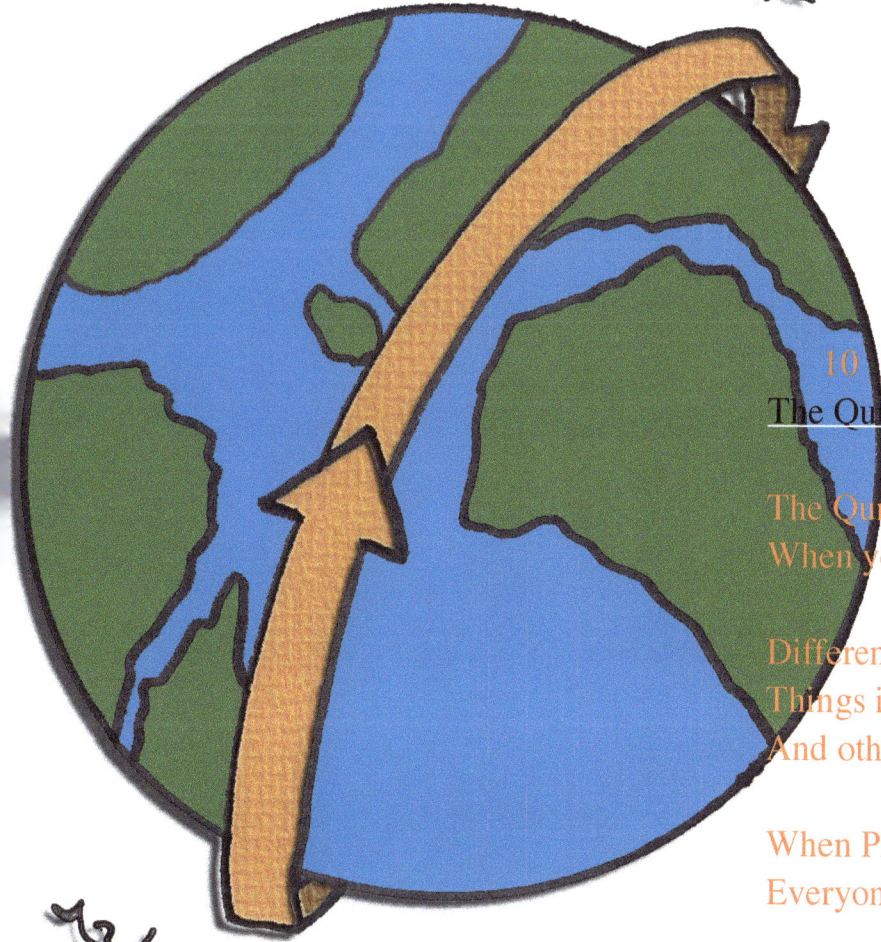

عمّ يتساءلون

عبس وتولّى

والعاديات ضبحًا

قل هو الله أحد

10
The Quran

The Quran is the book of guidance,
When you hear it, you will hear complete silence.

Different noises in the air,
Things in the Quran that will make you care,
And other things that will raise your hair.

When Prophet Mohamed revealed the Quran,
Everyone called it Al Furqan.

When spreading the Quran you will feel inspired,
After that you might feel very tired.

11
The Quran

The Quran is the words of Allah.

Read it and you'll please Allah.

It was revealed to Prophet Mohamed,
He is our messenger and our Prophet.

The Quran tells us right and wrong,
It is called the Furqan.

By: Rezwan Kabir

12
The Quran

The Quran is the guidance of Allah.

It contains many laws.

It hasn't any flaws.

The Quran brings us near,
So we shouldn't fear.

The Quran is a gift to us,
So we shouldn't fuss…about the truth.

Truly are we then Muslims…are you?

13
The Quran

The Quran is a book of Allah,
It tells us divine laws.

The Quran is a book of life,
It teaches us how to be nice.

The Quran helps us when we are in need,
It is the best gift indeed.

The book of Allah revealed to Rasool Allah,
Is a complete book of life here and after this life.

The poor and the rich need to learn,
Not to cheat, but to work to earn.

14
The Quran

The Quran talks about the bees.

It also talks about the trees.

It talks about the day and night.

It talks about the morning light.

It judges between right and wrong.

It's 114 chapters long.

Allah sent down the Quran in the holy month of Ramadan.

By: Hakim Kebir

15
Quran Poem

The Quran is our booklet.

No one can cook it.

Allah sent it to guide our kind.

Allah cares for mankind.

16
The Quran

Q is for quality.

U is for unique.

R is for the religion of Islam.

A is for Arabic.

N is for ninety-nine names of Allah.

Ramadan

17
Ramadan

Ramadan is a Holy month,
The Holy Quran was revealed in it.

It is the best,
And it is a test.

Allah tests you in this month.

He tests you on how much faith you have in Him,
And how much you can do for him like fasting and praying.

This tells you almost everything about Ramadan.

By: Sumayya Hussaini

18
Ramadan Poem

I fast from dawn to sunset.

I fast in Ramadan.

I wake up for Suhur and have time to eat Iftar.

I will be very patient.

I will be very good.

I will try my very best to make my fast good.

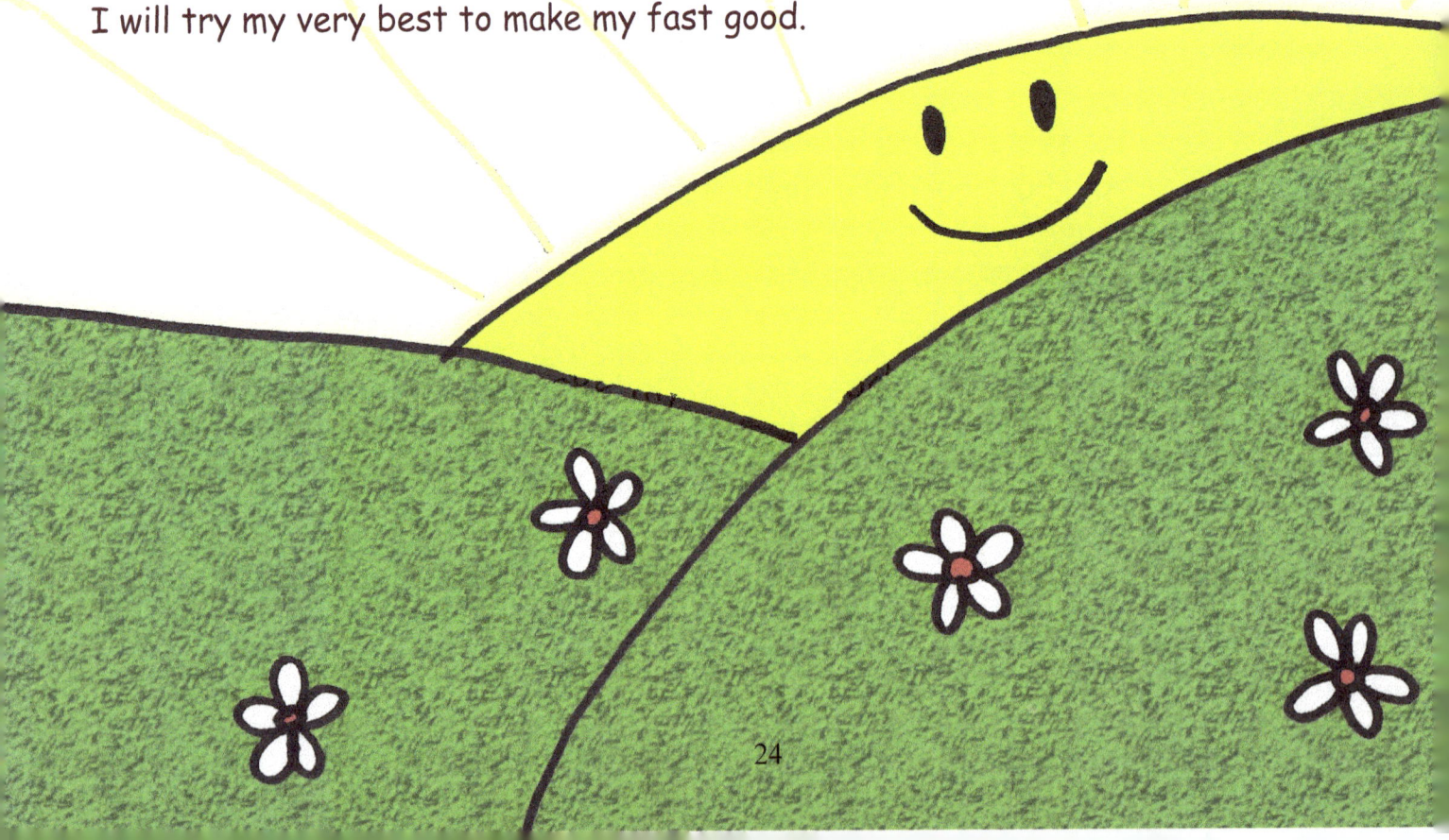

24

19

<u>Fasting</u>

Ramadan is the month of fasting,
And casting all the good qualities.

Fasting teaches us many things like:
Responsibility, patience, kindness, respect, obedience, praising Allah,
self-restraint, generosity, helpfulness, love and many more good qualities.

Could you think of more?

By: Sumayya Hussaini

Ramadan

In Ramadan we should fast,
Just like the people in the past.

We should fast from dawn to dusk,
Which means we shouldn't eat food like corn out of the husk.

We shouldn't drink water,
Even if you have a thirsty daughter.

When we break our fast we should eat dates,
A plate or two, but not a crate.

This is how we fast,
I hope it lasts.

21
Ramadan

Ramadan is when people give Zakat to the poor,
If you did not give enough you better give more.

Ramadan is when you fast,
If you do you will complete your task.

Ramadan is when you are kind,
Then you close your eyes and relax your mind.

22
The Ramadan Poem

Ramadan is a month of fasting.

Ramadan is a month of patience.

Ramadan is a month,
in which we have to control our anger.

Ramadan is a month,
that is better than a hundred months.

Ramadan is holy and blessed.

By: Sufian Hussaini

23
Ramadan

Ramadan is the month of blessing.

The month of fasting to please Allah.

We have a meal called Suhur to start our fast.

Then we have a meal called Iftar.

By: Hirra Shahid

24

Ramadan

In the month of Ramadan,
What was revealed is the Quran or the Furqan.

When we eat Suhur,
We must think of the poor.

If we fast,
Our good deeds will last.

We stay away from drink and food,
By the end of the month we'll be in a good mood.

By: Hadeer Soliman

25
<u>Ramadan Poem</u>

Ramadan is the month which you have to fast.

Be sure you don't eat breakfast, dinner or lunch.

Break your fast at the right time.

If you're really really hungry,
Then you might end up eating up a lime.

Congratulate yourself for getting through the day,
And thank Allah for not turning it grey.

26
<u>Ramadan</u>

In Ramadan we read the Quran.

In Ramadan we fast from dawn.

In Ramadan we say our prayers.

In Ramadan Muslims come together and unite.

27
Ramadan

Ramadan was the time the Quran was sent down,
Through Angel Gabriel to Prophet Mohamed and on to town.

Ramadan is the time to fast,
Because of the past,
It is not such a great task.

Ramadan is the time to give to the poor and needy,
Not to be greedy.

Ramadan is the time to pray,
Not to get you out from working all day.

By: Nabeeha Aleem

28

<u>In Ramadan</u>

In Ramadan we fast,
Some couldn't last.

We pray Salat Al Taraweeh and Witr,
We shouldn't litter.

We read the Quran at night,
But we should open the light.

By: Rizan Aziman

29

Ramadan Poem

Ramadan is the month of fasting,
It is not the month of lasting.

We do this to please Allah,
Just as we pray Salat.

My parents fast everyday,
Breaking their fast with a tray.

I am going to fast,
Just like the people of the past.

30
Ramadan

Ramadan is here,
You don't have to fear.

You pray more,
And give more.

So come to the mosque to break your fast with a date,
Don't be late.

And now it is time to break your fast,
At last!

Prophet Mohamed

Peace Be Upon Him

31
Prophet Mohamed

Kindest man you can find.

He always was in spite of the hardship he had known.

In oneness he believed and to us he preached.

By: Hadeer Soliman

32
Prophet Mohamed

M is for the messenger of Allah.

O is for outstanding.

H is for honorable.

A is for amiable.

M is for marvelous.

E is for excellent.

D is for devoted to Allah.

By: Sumayya Hussaini

33
Prophet Mohamed

The Prophet is nice,
The Prophet is kind.

If you follow him,
He will lead you to the right side.

The Prophet is great,
If you meet him you will know.

He is the best of mankind.

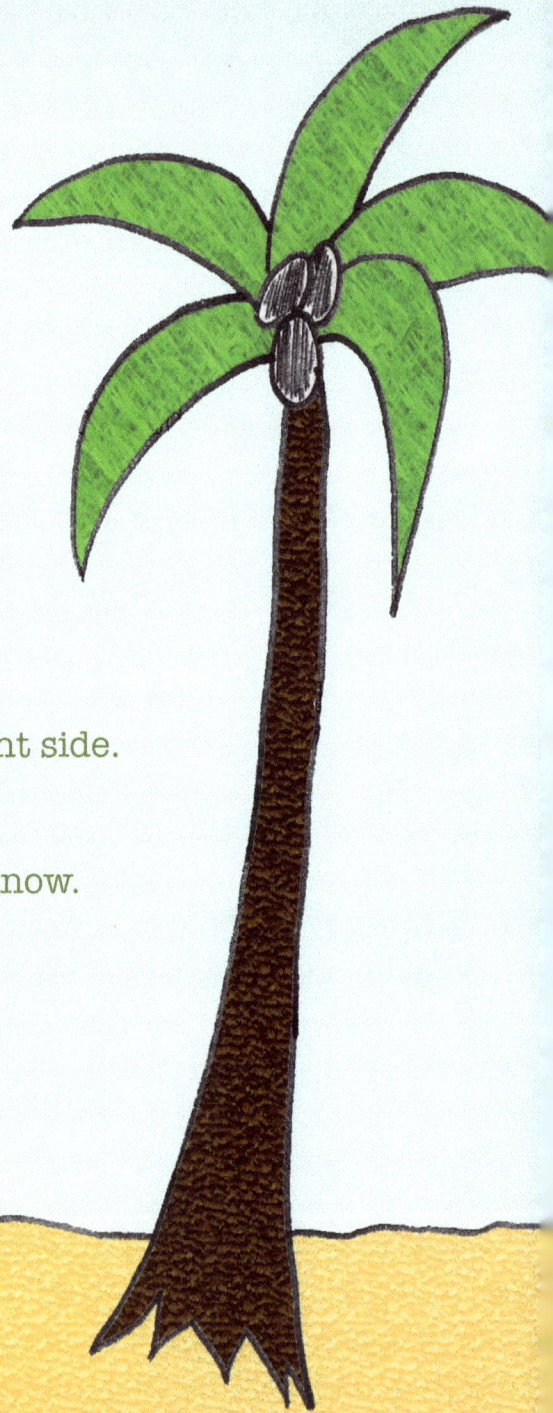

34
Prophet Mohamed

Prophet Mohamed is Allah's Prophet.

He is the last Prophet on earth.

Prophet Mohamed is a kind Prophet.

Just like the other Prophets.

Prophet Mohamed teaches Islam.

His followers are called Muslims.

Prophet Mohamed is called Al Amin.

It means he is the trustworthy one.

35
Prophet Mohamed

Prophet Mohamed is kind.

The greatest man of mankind.

Prophet Mohamed is the messenger of Allah.

And very, very talented.

By: Nabeeha Aleem

Eid

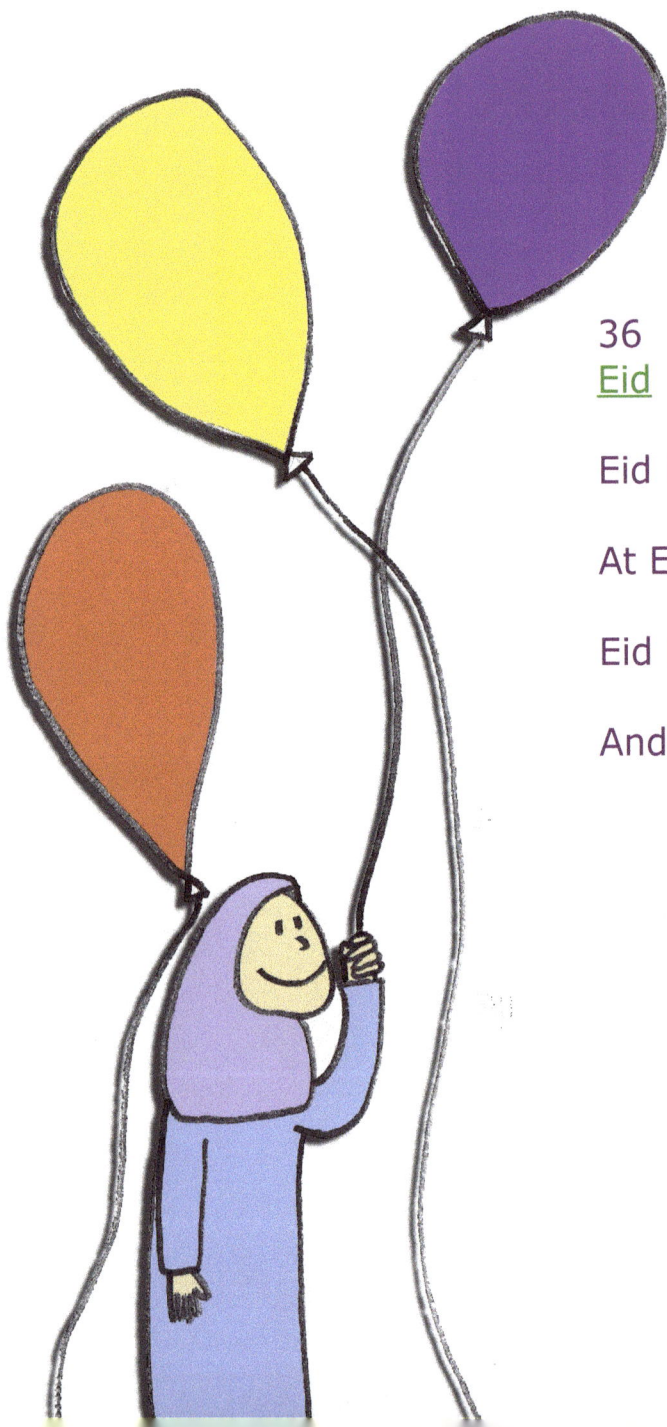

36
Eid

Eid is fun.

At Eid we pray.

Eid is rest.

And Eid is the best.

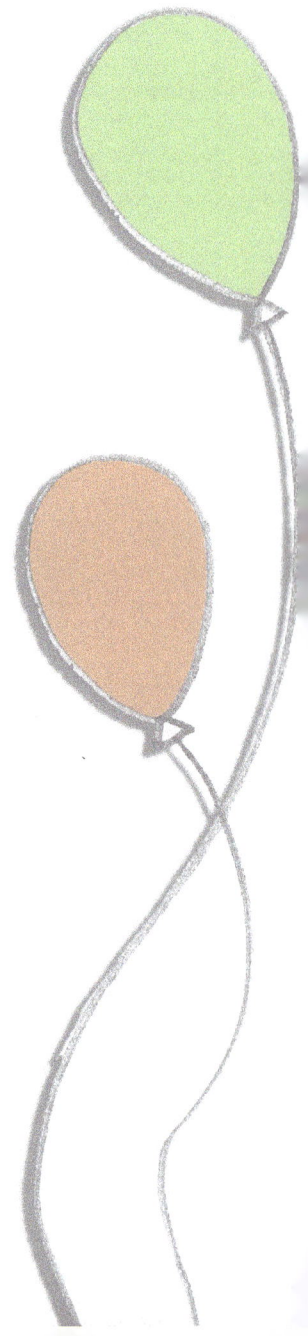

37
Eid

Eid is charmful but not harmful.

Eid is a day that is a money day.

In Eid you get many gifts and yummy crisps.

If you don't celebrate Eid it is no bad deed.

But you should if you could.

In Eid you should give, give and give,
Because Allah said the more you give the more you get.

By: Sumayya Hussaini

EID MUBARA[K]

38
<u>Eid</u>

The Quran is what I read in Eid.

Fitr is its last name.

But it isn't lame.

They give money to me.

They even make me responsible for the house key.

I give some people a giant gift.

But I need my friends to help me lift.

By: Rizan Aziman

HAPPY EID

39
Eid

Eid is when I feel the need to do a good deed.

Eid is when I help the poor if they show up at my door.

Eid is when I give money, which is very sunny.

Eid is when Muslims get together even in good or bad weather.

Eid is when no one is mad even when it is bad.

Eid is to worship only the one God.

By: Nabeeha Aleem

40
Eid Poem

Eid is the time when you have fun.

And is the time where you enjoy and play under the sun.

You get presents and toys.

You get to learn how to play with girls and boys.

Don't be greedy and always expecting to get gifts.

Be like the people who are planning to give and make lists.

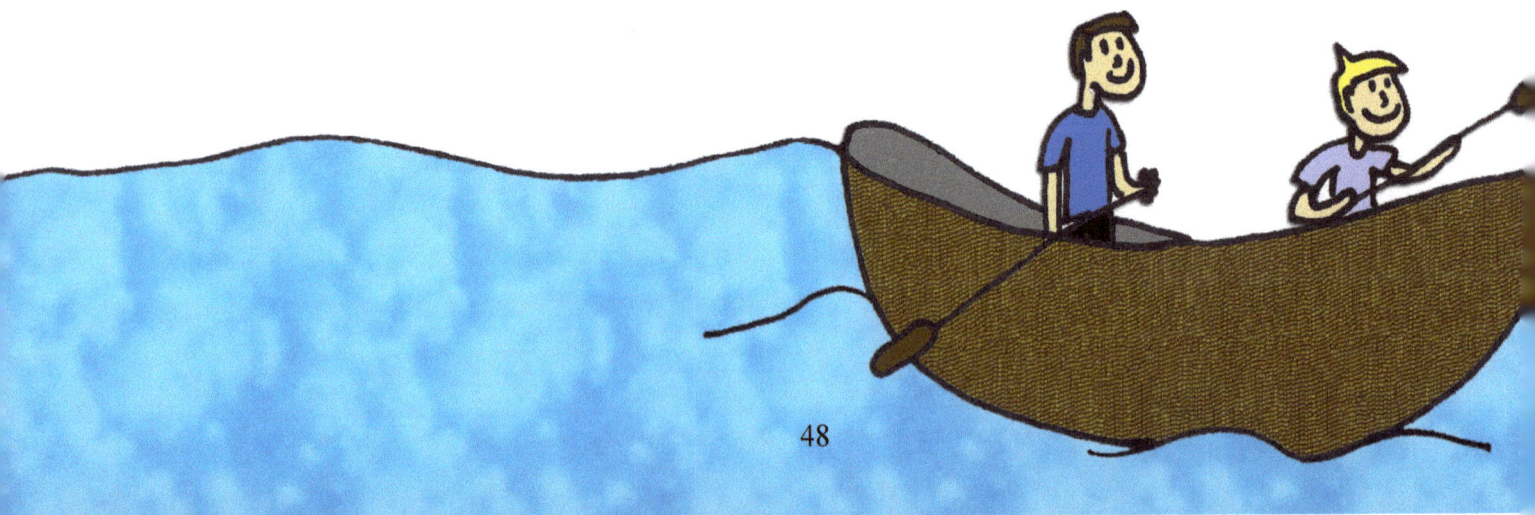

eid mubarak

41
Eid

In Eid we feed the people who need.

We have prayer together in mosques then we go to parks.

Eid, Eid, Eid Saeed.

After Ramadan we can eat all the good food and sweets.

As you can see Eid is always good with the family.

We exchange the gifts that we can buy like maybe even a tie.

And this is the end of my rhyme for this time.

By: Hadeer Soliman

42
Eid

In Eid we pray.

And we play.

We have fun in the house.

We make sure there is not one mouse.

We eat and have fun in the sun.

By: Janna Soliman

Thankfulness

43
Thankfulness

I am thankful for my dad,
Who never gets mad.

I am thankful for my mom,
Who makes me happy when I frown.

I am thankful for my sister,
Who likes me forever.

I am thankful for my family,
Who all love me happily.

By: Nabeeha Aleem

44
Poem on Thankfulness

Be thankful for your parents,
Be thankful for your friends.

Be thankful you've got many things,
Or you'll be one of the greedy men.

Some people may be rich,
Some people may be poor.

Be thankful you've got something,
And of course I won't forget Allah because He is just the best.

And this is where my poem comes to an end,
I hope you enjoyed this poem my friends.

45

Thankfulness

Thank you Allah for everything you've given me and everything you will give me.

Thank you for giving me loving and caring parents.

Thank you for giving me food to eat and drinks to drink.

Thank you for the health and wealth you've given to me.

I am grateful and thankful for everything.

Thank you.

By: Sumayya Hussaini

Thankfulness Poem

I thank Allah.

I thank my parents.

I thank my friends.

For all they have given.

I thank them very much.

For all they have done for me.

Be Thankful

Be thankful for each new challenge.

Be thankful for your mistakes.

Be thankful for when you are tired.

Because it is easy to be thankful.

For what you have made.

48

Thankfulness

We should be thankful for what we have.

For the senses Allah gave us: hearing, seeing, smelling, tasting and touching.

He gave us eyes that we blink and a brain for us to think.

If we believe in Allah we should not fear, he gave us the ear so we can hear.

I can see colors like black and white.

I thank Allah for my sight.

Thank you Allah very much for my hands, with which I can touch.

Thank you for the blessing of taste, you told us to be moderate, not to waste.

By: Hadeer Soliman

I am Thankful For...

49
Be Thankful

Be thankful, be thankful,
For Allah is so helpful.

He made the light,
That is so bright.

He gave you mom and dad,
They never make you sad.

Be thankful, be thankful,
For everything is colorful.

By: Rizan Aziman

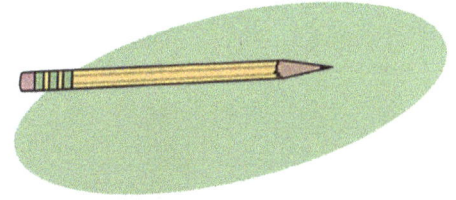

50

What am I Thankful for?

Thanks to my eyes,
I can see what flies in the skies.

Thanks to my ears,
I have no fears.

Thanks to my schools,
That taught me the rules.

Thanks to my parents who are wise,
They tell me to say no lies,

Thanks to my parents who take me to the park,
Even in the dark.

By: Hadeer Soliman

$$4 \times 3 = 12$$

Some of the young writers now...

Rezwan Kabir was a Civil Engineering student at the University of California, Irvine. He was an active member of and helps coordinate events for the Campuswide Honors Student Council and the Muslim student organization. He plans on going on to graduate school to pursue a Master's in Structural Engineering. In his free time, he enjoys watching movies, playing videogames, and hanging out with his friends. He considers Islam to be a fundamental part of his life as he continues his ongoing goal to learn about Islam and better himself as a Muslim.

Hirra Shahid currently lives in Los Angeles, CA. She studied economics at the University of Southern California. Hirra plans to attend business school in the future. In her free time, she enjoys reading and traveling.

Sufian Hussaini was a student at the University of California, Los Angeles. He was a History major with an Accounting minor. He aspires to be an investment banker and an exemplary Muslim.

Some of the young writers now...

Hadeer Soliman was a senior Public Health Science and Spanish double major at the University of California, Irvine. She was an active member of the Muslim student organization and a member of the Campuswide Honors Program. She plans to go to graduate school to eventually be able to benefit the community through health communication and education. She still loves writing in her free time and is an active member of the Muslim community in Southern California.

Hakim Kebir was a student at the University of California, Irvine. He was a Biology major student and enjoys basketball and volunteering in his free time. He aspires to be a doctor and hopes to be able to benefit Muslim youth with his work.

Janna Soliman attended Northwood High School in Irvine, CA. She is active with the Muslim Student Association and the youth group within the Muslim community.

Additional Thanks:

Marya Bangee
Ibrahim Ashmawey

www.ingramcontent.com/pod-product-compliance
Lightning Source LLC
Chambersburg PA
CBHW041635040426

42447CB00021B/3495